A Ship to Hold the World

and

The Marionette's Ascent

A Double Volume of Poetry

Annabelle Moseley

Wiseblood Books

Milwaukee

Copyright © 2014 by Annabelle Moseley and Wiseblood Books
Published by Wiseblood Books
www.wisebloodbooks.com

Cover: Dominic Heisdorf

Printed in the United States of America
Set in Arabic Typesetting

Library of Congress Cataloging-in-Publication Data
Moseley, Annabelle, 1979-
A Ship to Hold the World and The Marionette's Ascent / Annabelle Moseley;
1. Moseley, Annabelle, 1979-
2. Poetry

ISBN-13: 978-0692290002
ISBN-10: 0692290001

Like a sumptuous Northern diptych—Van Eyck's *Crucifixion* and *Last Judgment*, say—Annabelle Moseley's twinned volumes treat Biblical subjects through stunning compositions and vivid colors. In *A Ship to Hold the World*, Old Testament voices speak from the embers of ancient narratives with a contemporary spark. In *The Marionette's Ascent,* it is not Dante who makes this spiritual journey but our *semblable*, a puppet, dancing to another's tune: we are all, at times, willing or unwilling marionettes, the book suggests, and who of us cannot feel the truth of this. Moseley pulls the strings in these signal volumes, and the resulting show is mesmerizing.

—David Yezzi

When we pray, we put our two hands together, a symbolic gesture made possible because our bodies rhyme. In this amazing collection, Annabelle Moseley has hinged together two books, which, on first glance, would seem to be very different than our matching hands: venerable voices from the Old Testament in the first book, followed by the far more contemporary voice of "Marion," a highly opinionated stringed puppet who has "dropped the ette" from her name. Moseley is a master of music in both volumes. Her characters speak in a perfect pentameter line, unnoticed because flawless. This poet knows line breaks: when to enjamb and when not. So never do we get the "Hallmark Card" effect. Instead, these are living voices we can really believe. "It's dancing through restraint that is the test," says Marion, and Annabelle Moseley has done just that in these remarkable poems.

—Bruce Guernsey

Reading Annabelle Moseley's double volume is like witnessing a dazzling, sophisticated "Cirque du Soleil" act. All elements combine; entertaining and strange, full of character and choreography, feeling and forward motion. There is never a dull moment, nor any passage which may be lightly-treated except to the reader's disadvantage. Good judgment is here, too, in great quantities, as though the poems of A Ship to Hold the World, and The Marionette's Ascent launched themselves from the flying trapeze of utterly-candid innocence, to fill the reader with trepidation, sailing over the safety net to safely land on a high platform of Wisdom—far above the reader, but visible, still.
—Jennifer Reeser

Annabelle Moseley's double gift of poetry (two books in one) is attuned to the higher powers that animate her art. Moseley's confidence in forms yields a voice that is, by turns, playful, darkly witty, passionate, and powerful. This poet breathes life into old toys and ancient texts, in the most serious kind of play: the artist's conjuring of worlds we can't resist.
—Ned Balbo

For my mother, Annabelle Moseley Rufino

CONTENTS

A Ship to Hold the World

Acknowledgments:

Able Muse: "Cain at The Potter's Wheel"

Dappled Things: "Delilah's Defense"
"Job at the Garage Sale"
"Hannah in the Waiting Room"
"How to Rise from The Dead"
"How to Go Like Lazarus"
"The Sacrifice"

Lucid Rhythms: "Leah, on The Analyst's Couch"
"Rachel, on Her Anniversary"
"Villanelle for Jephthah's
Daughter"

Measure: "Eden's Serpent in Vegas"

Mezzo Cammin: "Job Addresses God"
"God Answers Job"
"Rebekah Speaks of Jacob"
"Salome's Crown for John"

Seat of Wisdom: "Moses"
"Tobit's Will"
"Jacob Wrestles With It All"
(Published as "The Embrace")

The Lyric:	"The Whisper"
The Nervous Breakdown:	"Potiphar Tees Off"
The Seventh Quarry:	"David Runs Jonathan's Race"
	"The Scapegoat's Dream"
Verse Wisconsin:	"Noah"
Victorian Violet Journal:	

"Rondeau for Sarah's Garden"
"Naomi's Song for Ruth"
"Tobiah and Sarah: How to
Marry Death"

The following poems are reprinted with permission, originally published in "The Clock of the Long Now" (2012, David Robert Books)

"Job Addresses God"
(Published as "A Time to Rend")
"God Answers Job"
(Published as "A Time to Sew")
"Jacob Wrestles With It All"
(Published as "A Time To
Embrace")

I

Eden's Serpent in Vegas

"Now the serpent was the most cunning of all the animals..." (Gen 3:1)

Do you like cards? Let's play. Draw up a chair.
I always bite the Queen of Hearts for luck.
You see her dog-eared King there? What a pair.
Sometimes my spittle stays; I get them stuck
before I cut the deck, and you'll observe
they rarely end up in the same hand. Fold.
I almost always win. That's why you'll serve
me playing straight or cheating. Oh, it's old,
explaining how I know the braille of lies—
twitch, scratch, the way the players move their hands.
I tell you that it isn't in the eyes.
Before you reach, I can predict your plans.
Desire trembles in the fingers first.
Your thumbs betray your longing. So, you're cursed.

This game is more than allegorical.
It's said that some can sense a coming rain
within their joints. My skin's an oracle
that way. I shed my memories, slough the pain
of all my patients, as I deal and bluff.
You can't imagine all the fools I've healed.
I'm told that my prescriptions can be tough.
I've always dealt out honesty, revealed

the truth, as with my infamous first play.
Speaking of rain, the garden was slick-wet
the day I whispered to her. To obey
without first tasting brings about regret.
She learned that from me. So did he. Death's small
compared to knowledge. Fold now. Touch me. Fall.

A Hebrew word for serpent is nachash, *associated with fortune-telling, divination, thus at home with card-play. It is said that the serpent had legs and perhaps even dragon-like wings prior to the Fall of Adam and Eve, and as punishment for tempting the humans, God decided: "On your belly you shall crawl, and dirt shall you eat all the days of your life." (Gen 3:14)*

Cain at the Potter's Wheel

"The Lord then said: 'What have you done! Listen: your brother's blood cries out to me from the soil!'" (Gen 4:10)

We never knew the garden, only clay
of life in exile. Between the knees
of Eve we were born—spinning in the gray
formation of her wheel. She tried to squeeze
our open mouths until each was a vase—
open to what she poured—twin vessels of
right judgment, holders of good speech. She'd glaze
our cries by coating them with words like love
and bringing stolen flowers and cut fruit
from someplace far away. And *I* always
asked where they came from. Taken with the root
of things, I used their seeds to fill my days
and grew a new garden for Adam, Eve—
a paradise they wouldn't have to leave.

A paradise they wouldn't have to leave,
I thought. I offered my best crops to Eve—
but they were tinged with Eden. Adam grieved,
refusing to eat memories. Abel's sleeve
was stained with blood, the slaughter. But they'd eat
what *he* brought home. It was the same with God.
They all preferred the dead lamb to the wheat

and so I hit the butcher with my rod
and planted him—the broken shards, to see
what he would grow. Nothing, nothing, nothing.
No rose to make Eve smile, not a tree
to root Adam from leaving—not a ring
to join mother and father—just the sound
of Abel's blood, crying beneath the ground.

Delilah's Defense

I.

And I cut off the hair that was his strength.
It was as if he knew I'd cause his end.
Persistently I asked what weary length
someone would need to go to, to suspend
his Herculean strength. And what he said—
I did. He said if he were tied with string
he'd be weak as a child. I tried; he shed
the shackles. Then he claimed rope was the thing
to bind him. I kept asking him to tell
the truth, confide in me. I pressed him. And
he must have noticed that I plotted hell,
betrayal. Every time he spoke, I planned.
He had to see that what he'd say, I'd do.
It was a game to him. It was my coup.

II.

It was a game to him. It was my coup.
I'd tired of his swagger and his brawn—
As if he never had a mother, drew
no strength from her milk, as if every dawn
he didn't rise from me renewed, as though
all he had poured within me had not shed
his burdens—fears, and loneliness—the show
of being unassailable. He said
he loved me. But there was a line of girls
before me. All of them ended up dead—
killed by his enemies. Though they were pearls,
he spoke of them as empty shells instead.
I think he always knew what I would do.
It was a game to him. It was my coup.

III.

It was a game to him. It was my coup.
How many times he'd told me stories of
the lion that he'd slaughtered, ripped in two.
How could a man like that return my love?
What made me think he'd ever understand?
At first, I thought attraction, passion, sex
could bond the space between us. Just his tanned
and muscled body made me think each flex
was meant for me. He was so much the man.
But surely someone womanly as I
could soften him, could lift his senseless ban
on tenderness. He said he'd rather die.
I waited for his sensitive debut.
It was a game to him. It was my coup.

IV.

It was a game to him. It was my coup.
Do you know, when he passed the lion's corpse—
later that day, he found a sweetened brew
inside its carcass? His luck boggles, warps
my thoughts. He reached within, ate honey from
the very thing he'd killed. The cloying truth?
He used to call me "honey," run his thumb
along my thigh. A powerful sweet tooth
my lover had—and so to please him, fruit
each night after he'd have me. Such a sweet,
sweet Samson would appear behind the brute.
And so I started planning his defeat.
He had to know that I would be untrue.
It was a game to him. It was my coup.

V.

It was a game to him. It was my coup.
He knew his strength supreme, no man could stop
his power. So what could a woman do?
Confession was his challenge to me. *Chop
my hair and I'll be helpless*, he said, but
had really come to think that it was he,
not his long, sacred hair that let him strut
around, to threaten men, watch children flee.
They were all Philistines. My people. Mine.
He killed a thousand of them with a bone,
the jawbone of an ass. What sort of shrine
can you provide the victims who were shown
such little mercy? Mocked. Slain. What to do?
It was a game to him. It was my coup.

VI.

It was a game to him. It was my coup.
It's true that I was offered silver, that
eleven hundred shekels waited—true
there must have been a bit of greed, some fat,
slovenly greed within me to accept
a price for what I did. He'd killed my friend,
my brother, several cousins. Still I slept
with him, and loved him once. But in the end
I hated how he boasted of his might.
He spoke of *men* he'd killed as though a herd
of *animals* he'd slain. And at first light,
he'd rise and leave without a tender word.
It's true that I accepted silver. True.
It was a game to him. It was my coup.

VII.

It was a game to him. It was my coup.
But if I wanted justice, why then take
pay for the man who'd killed my people? Few
would have the strength to spy, sleep with the snake.
And yet, I loved him when he was asleep.
When all his bragging, swaggering was done.
He was so handsome. Sometimes I would weep.
I was a fool. He looked just like the sun.
Bronze skin, gold flecks in his brown mane.
I was a bitch. He trusted like a boy.
How could I plan against him, cause him pain?
He was a murderer. I was his toy.
Sometimes I think that Samson killed me, too.
It was a game to me. It was his coup.

Lot's Tribute

"The sun was just rising over the earth as Lot arrived in Zoar; at the same time the Lord rained down sulphurous fire on Sodom and Gomorrah...But Lot's wife looked back, and she was turned into a pillar of salt." (Gen 19:23-24, 26)

This shot is for my wife. Bartender, salt.
Rim this thumb with that mineral of tears,
the only kiss she'll give me now. The fault
was hers for looking back, and all those years
of adding salt to food. A heavy hand
she had, a heavy everything, in fact.
Listen, it isn't like her end was planned
by me. And now my city has been sacked.
So here's to Noah. Why? He did it right.
That bad-ass fled destruction like a king,
his ship beat back the brackish waves of fright.
I ran like a buffoon to flee the sting
of sulfurous fire. My wife is toast.
Noah towed all the world to safety's coast.

Noah towed all the world to safety's coast.
Sulfurous fire came. My wife is toast.
I ran like a buffoon to flee the sting;
his ship beat back the brackish waves of fright.
That bad-ass fled destruction like a king;
So here's to Noah. Why? He did alright

by me. But now my city has been sacked.
Listen, it's not like my wife's end was planned.
She had a heavy everything, in fact—
was always adding salt. A heavy hand
was hers for looking back on all those years.
The only kiss she'll give is brined with fault.
Rim this thumb with that mineral of tears.
This shot is for my wife. Bartender, salt.

Leah, On the Analyst's Couch

"Jacob had fallen in love with Rachel...served seven years for [her], yet they seemed to him but a few days because of his love for her...Laban invited all the local inhabitants and gave a feast. At nightfall he took his daughter Leah and brought her to Jacob, and Jacob consummated the marriage with her...In the morning, Jacob was amazed: it was Leah! So he cried out to Laban: 'How could you do this to me! Was it not for Rachel that I served you? Why did you dupe me?" (Gen 29:18, 20, 22-23, 25)

You know the ones who seem to have it all—
the ones born shining, musical and smart?
My sister's one of those made to enthrall.
Hardest to take? She's also got a heart
which makes her hard to hate. I manage, though.
When she was young she toddled after me.
We're aging. I'm like gin. She's sweet bordeaux...
Do you say anything besides: *I see?*
What are you jotting? Grocery lists? Hangman?
I wonder if you're writing that I'm nuts.
But I was overlooked; I had to plan.
My sister has the looks; I've got the guts.
I will not tell you I regret the prize.
I took her man. His trust was my disguise.

I took her man. His trust was my disguise.
I will not tell you I regret the prize.
My sister has the looks; I've got the guts.

But I was overlooked; I had to plan.
I wonder if you're writing that I'm nuts.
What are you jotting? Grocery lists? Hangman?
Do you say anything except: *I see?*
We're aging. I'm like gin. She's sweet bordeaux.
When she was young she toddled after me,
which makes her hard to hate. I manage, though.
Hardest to take? She's also got a heart.
My sister's one of those made to enthrall:
the ones born shining, musical and smart—
you know, the ones who seem to have it all.

Rachel, on Her Anniversary

"Jacob...finished the bridal week for Leah, and then Laban gave him his daughter Rachel in marriage...Jacob then consummated his marriage with Rachel also, and he loved her more than Leah." (Gen 29:28, 30)

I'm envy's pearly mollusk. Hear my wail.
But wait, you can't. My mouth's shelled like a snail,
for my first wedding night was stolen. Wine
was poured as Jacob danced, entrapment's twine—
Old Leah in my place; she wore the veil.

He cried out for my breasts. Her nubs were frail.
My mouth held passion's flush; her lips were pale.
In bed, I was a spark. She lay supine.
I'm envy's pearly mollusk.

Jacob and I were trapped in Father's jail,
beauty and patience serving as my bail.
I told myself our love was more divine
and slept alone, consoled by stolen wine,
consigned to father's plans, desire's sale.
I'm envy's pearly mollusk.

Potiphar Tees Off

"Now Joseph was strikingly handsome in countenance and body. After a time, [Potiphar's] wife began to look fondly at him and said, 'Lie with me.'" (Gen 39:6-7)

Hey, Caddy, what's your name? You drag your feet.
My grip is off today. Hazards abound.
This course is challenging. I'll have to cheat.
My wife would know about that. Turn around.
I don't like being watched when I chicane.
Hand me that iron for my uphill lie.
I've never liked this fairway; what a pain.
How much pay would you need to be a spy?
Drive over to the pool; you'll find her there.
She'll be in our cabana. You're her type.
Her golden limbs will be outstretched and bare,
her mouth a pouting peach, juicy and ripe.
Tell her she's gorgeous. She never hears me.
Then come right back in time for the next tee.

Then come right back in time for the next tee.
Tell her she's gorgeous. She never hears me.
Her mouth a pouting peach, juicy and ripe,
her golden limbs will be outstretched and bare—
she'll be in our cabana. You're her type.
Drive over to the pool; you'll find her there.
How much pay would you need to be a spy?

I've never liked this fairway; what a pain.
Hand me that iron for my uphill lie.
I don't like being watched when I chicane.
My wife would know about that. Turn around.
This course is challenging. I'll have to cheat.
My grip is off today. Hazards abound.
Hey, Caddy, what's your name? You drag your feet.

The Sacrifice

"Then God said, 'Take your son Isaac, your only one, whom you love, and go to the land of Moriah. There you shall offer him up as a holocaust on a height that I will point out to you.'" (Gen 22:2)

"Thereupon Abraham took the wood for the holocaust and laid it on his son Isaac's shoulders, while he himself carried the fire and the knife...When they came to the place of which God had told him, Abraham built an altar and arranged the wood on it. Next he tied up his son Isaac, and put him on top of the wood on the altar. Then he reached out and took the knife to slaughter his son. But the Lord's messenger called to him from heaven, 'Abraham, Abraham...Do not lay your hand on the boy...Do not do the least thing to him. I know how devoted you are to God, since you did not withhold from me your beloved son.'" (Gen 2:6, 9-12)

I. Abraham Addresses God

You knew I would withhold nothing from you.
Why would you ask for me to kill my son?
What if he was your boy? What would you do?
Have you ever known pain? For I've begun
to question why you'd test me that way. He
was young, my only child, asked me where
we'd find the sheep to slay. He trusted me.
I still have dreams at night about my prayer—
to you—as I bound Isaac, as he cried—
I told you he was yours to take. I'd raised
that child—and now raised my knife. Provide
me with a reason. Was I numb? Or crazed?
I know your angel stopped me, God, but why
ask me to kill to prove that I'd comply?

II. God Answers Abraham

It is not disrespect to question me.
I saw the way that Sarah looked at you
when Isaac told her God had set him free.
She wondered if you would have followed through—
and killed her boy. But just as I gave birth
to Isaac with her help, I gave him life
again—through sparing him I taught the earth:
I don't want children carried to the knife.
Your Isaac bore the sacrificial wood
upon his back. But one day, Abraham,
I'll know your pain.   On that day I'll make good—
I'll give my sacrifice for you—my lamb;
carry, like wood, the pain that Isaac knew—
give what I wouldn't take away from you.

Rondeau for Sarah's Garden

"Now Abraham and Sarah were old, advanced in years...So Sarah laughed to herself and said, 'Now that I am so old, am I still to have...pleasure?'" (Gen 18:12)

Our hands anoint the dirt and cradle loam.
We plant to bless our bodies' final home.
We're more alive—producing cumin, sage.
Working the soil comforts our old age.
We edit weeds; each blossom is a poem.

The garden's our posterity, a tome
written in earth, impermanent as foam.
Our fingers unknot tendrils like a comb.
Our hands anoint the dirt.

Some evenings, stars and clouds provide a dome.
We plant to bless our bodies' final home.
Coupled like wheat and chaff, we love, assuage
the youthful longings held within the cage
of aging bodies. No more will we roam.
Our hands anoint the dirt.

The Scapegoat's Dream

"Israel [Jacob] loved Joseph best of all his sons, for he was the child of his old age; and he had made him a long tunic. When his brothers saw that their father loved him best of all his sons, they hated him so much that they would not even greet him." (Gen 37:3-4)

"'Come closer to me,' he told his brothers. When they had done so, he said: 'I am your brother Joseph, whom you once sold into Egypt.'" (Gen 45:4)

I didn't tell you, brothers, of the dreams
that came to me the night before you sold
and left me: My bright coat was torn, the seams
coated in blood, but all the blood was gold—
the color of Egyptian pyramids.
That motley coat—its patterned waves were froth
to me. I looked at it and saw the squid
of Father's pride, bright tentacles of cloth.
(To wear it was a risk, but if that man
had given me a coat of brush and thorns
I would have put it on.) It was my plan
to run. Then I saw two goats—all four horns
were red, each gleaming like a shining crown—
One ran into the desert, one fell down.

One ran into the desert, one fell down—
And as it died, my coat floated from reach,
surrendered all its colors—in the brown
trout-colored sands, then suddenly its peach,

like salmon, splashed into the morning sky—
its seaweed colors coated each of you.
I thought how beautiful, how like goodbye
your flesh looked—fronds of green—painted, tattooed.
The whale-blue seeped inside our father's skin
and settled in his veins like fraying silk.
Then I became a thrashing fish, each fin
severed at knifepoint; all my blood was milk.
You drank of it, and still I swam. I knew
what you would do; you made me what I am.

Once a year in ancient Israel a high priest would acquire two goats. One would be killed and its blood sprinkled in the temple. The other goat ritually carried the sins of the people and was sent off into the desert on the Day of Atonement. These sacrifices were offered to God as expiation for the transgressions of the Israelites.

Miriam Witnesses Moses' Adoption

"Now a certain man of the house of Levi married a Levite woman, who conceived and bore a son. Seeing that he was a goodly child, she hid him for three months. When she could hide him no longer, she took a papyrus basket, daubed it with bitumen and pitch, and putting the child in it, placed it among the reeds on the river bank. His sister stationed herself at a distance to find out what would happen to him." (Ex 2:1-4)

The river joined two women's gifts that day.
My baby brother floated in between
the strength to give a treasured son away

and courage of adoption. Crouched, unseen,
my long hair blending with the river reeds.
I bit my hand, afraid I'd intervene,

and shout to Pharaoh's daughter of his needs,
the way laughter could always soothe his cries,
the way he played with mother's wooden beads.

And as I watched, I slowly realized
it was as hard for that Princess to choose
to take him; as for us to compromise—

guarding his innocence from evil's sway.
The river joined two women's gifts that day.

Moses

"An angel of the Lord appeared to him in fire flaming out of a bush. As he looked on, he was surprised to see that the bush, though on fire, was not consumed...the Lord said, 'Come, now! I will send you to Pharaoh to lead my people, the Israelites, out of Egypt.'" (Ex 3:2, 10)

I was adopted from the river bank.
There's something to the way reeds sway in wind,
the way they lean down low—that makes me thank
the One who gave me life. Yet I rescind
the urge to make my home the water's edge—
though often in this desert all I see
are lotuses where sand should be, and sedge
instead of the occasional palm tree.
I tire of this desolation, miss
the structured boats, scaled pyramids, ripe trees.
But all I hear are crying babies, hiss
of camels. All around me: fear, unease.
How can I ever guide my people home,
when my spirit is trapped beneath the foam—

When my spirit is trapped beneath the foam,
beneath the Nile's cool and trickling waves?
I long for fertile banks, the rich, dark loam.
Out in this wasteland, all I see are graves.
The river is my lineage. And yet

there's something else that keeps me walking on.
I go because I'm paying off a debt
that never can be paid in full. Each dawn,
and every sunset, I become a reed
bowing in weariness. Why am I led
to thank this Wild Mystery? I need
my jealous God; the manna, desert bread—
the burning bush; the basket that held me
when I, an infant, floated helplessly.

Deborah's Apiary

"At this time the prophetess Deborah...was judging Israel. She used to sit under Deborah's palm tree...and there the Israelites came up to her for judgment." (Jgs 4:4-5)

The honey of an oracle can sting,
when you want sweet solution in a jar
and get instead a challenge that will cling.
You like the thought of channeling a star,
imagine that I'll chant and close my eyes.
When you ask me to judge what you should do,
you don't expect the flight path I advise.
You want to go around; I say, go through;
I've learned from bees. Profit begins as stain;
bring back your clinging pollen to the hive.
The amber nectar comes from work and pain.
You don't need cloying counsel. You need drive.
Only rapid wings buzz. You must move, fast.
Don't second-guess the battle. You will last.

Don't second-guess the battle. You will last.
Only rapid wings buzz. You must move, fast.
You don't need cloying counsel. You need drive.
The amber nectar comes from work and pain.
Bring back your clinging pollen to the hive.
I've learned from bees. Profit begins as stain.

39

You want to go around; I say, go through.
You don't expect the flight path I advise.
When you ask me to judge what you should do,
imagine that I'll chant and close my eyes.
You like the thought of channeling a star
and get instead a challenge that will cling;
when you want sweet solution in a jar,
the honey of an oracle can sting.

Deborah means 'bee' in Hebrew. This prophetess summoned her people to battle against invaders and wrote a victory song after the battle.

Naomi's Song for Ruth

"'Go back, my daughters!' said Naomi. 'Why should you come with me? Have I
other sons in my womb who may become your husbands?'...But Ruth said, 'Do not
ask me to abandon or forsake you! For wherever you go I will go, wherever you
lodge I will lodge, your people shall be my people, and your God, my God.'" (Ru
1:11-12, 16)
"Ruth the Moabite said to Naomi, 'Let me go and glean ears of grain in the field of
anyone who will allow me that favor.'" (Ru 2:2)

Wherever you go, I will go, she said.
Devotion like this I had never found
in any man—even my sons, now dead.
Not even at my husband's funeral mound
did anyone else comfort me this way.
The famine came, I lost them one by one.
And now a woman offered to repay?
Yet I had always thought that there were none
among women whom I could lean on, trust.
And now I had this daughter—stubborn, kind.
She wanted to grow barley from the dust.
To give me all the strength I had resigned,
my daughter-in-law filled her arms with grain—
to harvest me from fallow fields of pain.

To harvest me from fallow fields of pain,
my daughter-in-law filled her arms with grain—
to give me all the strength I had resigned.

She wanted to grow barley from the dust.
And now I had this daughter—stubborn, kind
among women, whom I could lean on, trust—
yet I had always thought that there were none.
And now a *woman* offered to repay.
The famine came. I lost them one by one.
Did anyone else comfort me this way?
Not even at my husband's funeral mound.
In any man—even my sons, now dead—
devotion like this I had never found.
Wherever you go, I will go, she said.

Hannah in the Waiting Room

"...if you give your handmaid a...child, I will give him to the Lord for as long as he lives." (1 Sm 1:11)

I'm through with waiting; when will my turn come?
The world is full of accidental birth
fermenting—sweet, astonishing as rum.

Such unplanned joy inebriates the earth.
Right now I'm drunk on emptiness, lost time—
an impulse tying motherhood to worth.

It's hard to win. Each way is like a crime.
A child so soon? Just one? No girl? No boy?
What are you waiting for? You're in your prime.

Soon everything reminds—each pram, each toy,
each baby blanket should be for my own.
Dear God, I will provide love, counsel, joy.

I beat this prayer out daily like a drum.
I'm through with waiting; when will my turn come?

Villanelle for Jephthah's Daughter

"Jephthah made a vow to the Lord. 'If you deliver the Ammonites into my power... whoever comes out of the doors of my house to meet me when I return in triumph from the Ammonites shall belong to the Lord. I shall offer him up as a holocaust.' When Jephthah returned to his house in Mitzpah, it was his daughter who came forth, playing the tambourines and dancing." (Jgs 11:30-31, 34)

I trusted innocence would shield my fate,
as though I wasn't born a flag for pain.
Like lines of girls before me, I was bait.

Iphigenia died, promised a mate.
Psyche was sacrificed, offered like grain.
I trusted innocence would shield my fate.

But who was I? What's virtue? What's so great
about allure? Safer to be dull, plain.
Like lines of girls before me, I was bait.

I should have run away. Why did I wait?
My freedom seemed less pressing in the rain.
I trusted innocence would shield my fate.

I did not know my father would equate
his loss of me with spiritual gain.
Like lines of girls before me, I was bait.

Why didn't I resist the cruel dictate?
Perhaps I'd grown accustomed to the chain.
I trusted innocence would shield my fate
Like lines of girls before me, I was bait.

Rebekah Speaks of Jacob

"Rebekah said to her son Jacob, 'Listen, I overheard your father tell your brother Esau, "Bring me some game and with it prepare an appetizing dish for me to eat, that I may give you my blessing with the Lord's approval before I die." Now, son, ...go to the flock and get me two choice kids. With these I will prepare an appetizing dish for your father, such as he likes. Then bring it to your father to bless you before he dies...let any curse against you, son, fall on me!"' (Gen 27:6-10, 13)

"Jacob departed...Then he had a dream: a stairway rested on the ground, with its top reaching to the heavens; and God's messengers were going up and down on it." (Gen 28:10, 12)

I knew it was not something he'd outgrow.
He was a fighter. Weak, the smaller twin,
my Jacob clutched his brother's heel at birth;
it was innate to strive, vital to win.
A stairway shadowed everything he did.
He lived to climb. The blessing was his due.
But when he ran away, some called him cursed.
Jacob will find a ladder to break through
the clouds until he claws at heaven—finds
a way to get a blessing right from God
Himself. That's how ambition is designed—
to keep on trying till you get the nod.
No parent can resist the child who tries—
and God's a parent. He'll hear Jacob's cries.

Jacob Wrestles With It All

"You shall no longer be spoken of as Jacob, but as Israel, because you have contended with divine and human beings and have prevailed." (Gen 32:29)

I stood and watched the fingertips of stars
above the Jabbok River on the night
before I saw my brother, faced the scars
of what I had supplanted: the birthright
and blessing owed to Esau. I recalled
my bright dream of God's ladder to the sky;
the way I'd grasped for glory since I crawled;
the way I'd reached my mother's birthing thigh
still clinging to my older brother's heel.
And as I stood alone before the dawn,
an angel came to wrestle with me, feel
my human arms resisting holy brawn.
Though crippled, I refused to let him go
until the angel promised to bestow...

A blessing. Why was it always this way?
Why did I fight for God's favor like this?
Why couldn't I just fold my hands and pray?
But there was something pleasing as a kiss
in struggling for what I wanted most.
The angel rose and gave consent and then
renamed me Israel. That's how the ghost

that was my guilt and pride was beaten. (When
I stood and limped away, I knew I'd seen
the hand of God and lived, carried the weight
of what I witnessed in my arms. The scene
of flailing beneath heaven would abate
my longing.) When I'd clutch my old disgrace
in Esau's arms, it would be to embrace.

David Runs Jonathan's Race

"How can the warriors have fallen—in the thick of the battle, slain upon your heights!" (2 Sm 1:25)

He entered this race months before he died
and dreamed of victory, of placing first.
I'll run for him—each step will be his stride.
And as the shot resounds, runners dispersed
along the trail, the sweat will be my tears.
I'll proudly wear his number on my back
on top of mine, to honor his lost years.
We ran together, Sundays, at the track—
He'd beat me by ten yards. My training failed.
He thought the world was something he could win.
I saw him fall but once. He still prevailed,
grinning at his sprained foot, his bloody skin—
reaching the finish line with a loud cry.
I never thought someone so strong would die.

I never thought someone so strong would die.
Reaching the finish line with a loud cry,
grinning at his sprained foot, his bloody skin—
I saw him fall but once. He still prevailed.
He thought the world was something he could win.
He'd beat me by ten yards. My training failed.
We ran together, Sundays, at the track.

On top of mine, to honor his lost years,
I'll proudly wear his number on my back.
Along the trail, the sweat will be my tears.
And as the shot resounds, runners dispersed,
I'll run for him—each step will be his stride.
He dreamed of victory, of placing first,
and entered this race months before he died.

Bathsheba

"One evening David rose from his siesta and strolled about on the roof of the palace. From the roof he saw a woman bathing, who was very beautiful. David had inquiries made about the woman and was told, 'She is Bathsheba, daughter of Eliam, and wife of Uriah the Hittite.' Then David sent messengers and took her. When she came to him, he had relations with her..."(2 Samuel 11:2-4)

I.

I saw him in the moonlight, on the roof,
three months before he ever noticed me.
And I ignored him, tried to be aloof—
to finish bathing before he could see
that I was there. My handmaid brought a screen
each time, for modesty. I thought it right.
But as I lingered, naked and unseen,
my thoughts would lie beside him in the night—
and neither of us slept. I bathed, he paced.
The hours were dark and warm. I wanted him.
One night I dreamed his kiss, thought how he'd taste;
I tried to drown desire with a swim.
And one night when my maid was ill I left
the screen open—a sweet, forbidden cleft.

II.

The screen open, a sweet, forbidden cleft,
I got out of the pool, glistening, wet,
and let my hair down from its pins. I left
my white robe lying on the ground, was set
on letting him see everything. I closed
my eyes and felt him staring, gently turned
and bent to reach my robe. Slow and composed,
I put it on and lingered, and returned
to his full view, but never did I show
I wanted him. I did not tie the sash
over my thighs. A breeze began to blow.
I bent down to the pool, prepared to splash
my face. Then suddenly, I heard a voice.
He said, *Now follow me. You have no choice.*

III.

He said, *Now follow me. You have no choice.*
I closed my robe and nodded, walked with him,
the servant—I tried not to smile, rejoice.
I tried to seem surprised, afraid and prim.
The servant left me in a tower room.
David was there. He said, *I'd like to look
more closely at you.* Like a nervous groom,
he cleared his throat. I noticed his hands shook.
His beauty made me tremble. He had killed
men with those hands, and written songs to God.
He opened my robe, touched me. I was thrilled.
I asked him if I should lie down. His nod
was like a whole note, eager as a psalm.
I was the prayer he pressed beneath his palm.

Tobit's Will

"If I saw one...who had died and been thrown outside the walls of Nineveh, I would bury him." (Tb 1:17)

A fish's gall brings sight back to my eyes.
I am Tobiah's father; death is near—
always, because whenever someone dies
in Nineveh, no matter if they're dear
to me or strange, when they are killed, and cast
outside to rot, by orders of the king,
I bury them by stealth. I am the last
to look at them before I pray and fling
earth over them. Always, beneath my nails,
the loam of secret funerals. Blindness comes.
I am its trout, my eyes covered with scales.
My son returns, touches my eyes. I view
his face. He wipes my weakness with fish oil—
returns me to my calling, to the soil.

Return me to my calling, to the soil.
A gravedigger's at home with earth and clay.
My bones will clothe the naked dirt. The hole
I'll fill is like a mouth; and I, the bread.
When you are old, you visualize your end.
But working with death long enough, I've learned
to see life there. Things sprout from what you tend.

I've pulled the weeds; I've planted. I have earned
an expectation that something will grow
from my life when my body's underground.
There'll be some mourning, planted in a row,
flowers of memories; but what's more sound
is how the ones I've taught live like I showed.
That is my monument: what I've bestowed.

Job at the Garage Sale

"Though he heap up silver like dust / and store away mounds of clothing, / What he has stored the just man shall wear / and the innocent shall divide the silver." (Jb 27:16-17)

Perhaps you'd reconsider what that's worth.
That is my wedding silver, dim with time.
One polishing will give a shining birth
to what has faded with neglect and grime.
What's that you ask? No, not divorce. She died.
That was my wife's vase. Sure, a dollar's fine.
That lamp could be repaired; I never tried.
The house is on the market. See the sign?
Dear God, they pick through memories like trash,
and point at what they want and bargain down.
They cart away my life for crumpled cash.
They spread news of foreclosure through the town.
Dear God, my brokenness is yours, in crumbs.
They are like ants, feeding, where forfeit comes.

They are like ants, feeding, where forfeit comes.
Dear God, my brokenness is yours, in crumbs.
They spread news of foreclosure through the town.
They cart away my life for crumpled cash,
and point at what they want, and bargain down.
Dear God, they pick through memories like trash.

The house is on the market. See the sign?
That lamp could be repaired; I never tried.
That was my wife's vase. Sure, a dollar's fine.
What's that you ask? No, not divorce. She died.
To what has faded with neglect and grime,
one polishing will give a shining birth.
That is my wedding silver, dim with time;
perhaps you'd reconsider what that's worth.

Job Addresses God

"Then Job began to tear his cloak and cut off his hair." (Job 1:20)

The silence is all. Though I want to split
the stillness of this day with fractured cries,
and tear this room apart, I will admit
that such a sundering would not be wise.
What would it do to shatter every dish,
or smash the vases, break each cup and bowl?
How would that change what I've begun to wish—
that I could go right back to being whole—
even if it meant forgetting you and
the great pain that loving you has brought? I—
I tore my hair today. You understand?
My clothing, too. I wait for you to cry
out, ask me not to harm myself. I won't.
But I know loneliness. And God, you don't.

God Answers Job

"Who is this that obscures divine plans with words of ignorance? / ... Where were you when I founded the earth?" (Job 38:2, 4)

You say I don't know loneliness. What, Job,
you've never seen the chasms between stars?
Observe the distance of your heart, then probe
yourself for answers. Look down at your scars.
You think I put them there, I know. But pain
is from your world, not mine. And all the while
I plan my entrance. Gardens all need rain
to raise their beauty. My plot grows a trial
of such deep suffering, the torn curtain
of a great temple will be how I rend
the earth of sleep. Sacrifice makes certain
a love that will not hesitate or end.
Mend yourself, now. Follow my command.
(I'm pierced in ways you'll never understand.)

The Whisper

"Then the Lord said, 'Go outside and stand on the mountain before the Lord; the Lord will be passing by.' A strong and heavy wind was rending the mountains and crushing rocks before the Lord—but the Lord was not in the wind. After the wind there was an earthquake—but the Lord was not in the earthquake. After the earthquake there was fire—but the Lord was not in the fire. After the fire there was a tiny whispering sound. When he heard this, Elijah hid his face in his cloak and went and stood at the entrance of the cave. A voice said to him, 'Elijah, why are you here?'" (1 Kings 19:11-13)

That's why it is important to be loud.
In order to avoid the questions, keep
the conscience muted, stay within the crowd.
Make sure you are exhausted before sleep.
Play music when you're by yourself,
and talk more than you listen. Talk much more.
Leave prayer like dust, collecting on the shelf.
Don't meditate. Don't contemplate. Don't bore.
Think only of how much there is to do.
Don't gaze too long at nature; it's a trap.
Clouds are redundant. Skies are often blue.
Why study them? You'll be labeled a sap.
Do not sit still for long, or what you fear—
it will come. When you're still, it will appear.

It will come. When you're still, it will appear.
That is because its hush is always there.

And it will ask you, Why? Why are you here?
Why were you born? It's like a kind of dare
that you will want to answer. Wish for fire—
for wind or for an earthquake—anything
to keep the whisper out. Lean on desire.
Don't sleep alone. Don't eat alone. Don't bring
attention to the silence. Block it out.
Don't answer it. That's when it starts, you know.
Question that you felt the whisper. Doubt.
Why are you here? Don't worry. Let it go.
The whisper is the source of change, the knife.
You must avoid it. Just like death. Or life.

Noah

"The Lord wiped out every living thing on earth: man and cattle, the creeping things and the birds of the air; all were wiped out from the earth. Only Noah and those with him in the ark were left." (Gen 7:23)

My ancestors are mute and all I know
of them are ancient spear tips—and the shards
of painted cups that still, while faded, glow
as though they held wine. Handed down, these guards
over my past talk wordlessly of death
and what has been consumed. Now as I build
a ship to hold the world, I hold each breath
before exhaling—for all who'll be killed—
even as a few fragments cling to life.
I'll keep those broken few, and artifacts
of all who came before. What of their strife?
What of their burial? Borne on our backs
we'll carry memories of tombs and graves
to salvage and replant beyond the waves.

To salvage and replant beyond the waves,
we carried memories of tombs and graves.
What of their burial? Borne on our backs
were all who came before. What of their strife?
I kept the broken few and artifacts
even as a few fragments clung to life.

Before exhaling—for all who were killed—
a ship to hold the world, I held each breath
within my body's boat. Consumed, I built
over my past, talked wordlessly of death
as though wine. What was left, I tried to guard
like painted cups, faded—the rainbow's glow.
I kept the ancient spear tips—and the shards.
My ancestors are mute. That's all I know.

Eden's Serpent Escapes *The World of Reptiles*, Bronx Zoo

"'The World of Reptiles is closed today,' a sign explaining the closing said. 'Staff observed an...Egyptian cobra missing from an off-exhibit enclosure on Friday.'"
-NY Times, March 27, 2011

I.

I've crawled away like every other time,
the posture of humility, my ace.
Some say it is my penance for a crime.
But staying low's a great way to save face.
They never notice I outlive them all.
I always slither off, return, escape.
One day I'll go for good, leave just a sprawl
of outer skin behind, an empty shape—
curled epidermis of my former self.
I am an artist of the dodge and tease—
The reason I submit to the glass shelf.
A true ecdysiast, I strip with ease.
My skin's the bluff—it's never in the game.
I reinvent myself; transcending shame.

II.

Snakes reconstruct themselves four times a year,
dislodge the scaly habit, thrash and dance.
Try it sometime: an antidote to fear,
for reinvention grants a second chance.
Know you can be a stripper when you want.
And if you do it with a sweet-tongued hiss,
it will be seen as beauty, not a flaunt.
A well-timed bite can bristle like a kiss.
Why do you leave your clothes upon the floor
after the passion, when you're coiled tight?
You are a different being than before.
You've tasted your desire. Want is right.
My zoo exhibit teaches this first truth.
Every escape I stage renews my youth.

III.

So when I leave the zoo, I go on tour.
I bite at the Big Apple where I can.
I love the lights of Times Square, greed's bright lure.
I ride the subways. Pleasure is my plan.
I'm helped by cynicism, jaded grit.
No one makes eye contact, and no one cares
if I am Satan, if I strike or spit.
I must admit, I did expect some stares.
It truly helps my cause that I'm not seen—
unnoticed, work my card tricks, whisper lies.
(These hip Manhattanites are pretty green).
I set them free from taboo and disguise.
I hope my motives will not be maligned.
Card players love to deal out to the blind.

II

Tobiah and Sarah: How to Marry Death

"Tobiah objected, however: 'Brother Azariah, I have heard that this woman has already been married seven times, and that her husbands died in their bridal chambers. On the very night they approached her, they dropped dead. And I have heard it said it was a demon who killed them.'" (Tb 6:14)

"Raphael said to him: '...So now listen to me, brother; do not give another thought to this demon, but marry Sarah. I know that tonight you will have her for your wife! When you go into the bridal chamber, take the fish's liver and heart, and place them on the embers for the incense. As soon as the demon smells the odor they give off, he will flee...Then...both of you...pray.'" (Tb 6:16-18)

I.

There's always something standing in the way—
some rough impediment you must admit,
an obstacle, a challenge, a delay.
Ready to strike or fearful to commit—
there's always something in the way of love.
And what is in the way is always death.
How well Tobiah knew this, dreaming of
Sarah, whose seven husbands lost their breath
forever, on their wedding night as she
sat waiting on the bed, cried, watched them fall.
Before the honeymoon, the devotee
was dead, face down, a disappointed sprawl
of lust unrealized. But Tobiah knew
the way to help her. He would follow through.

II.

The way to help her? He would follow through.
Truly, he wanted her for who she was—
a woman to support, not just subdue
her fiend. He longed for her, not just because
she was a widow with a gorgeous face—
but he loved her as family, like the wish
who had been set apart for him, by grace.
And so he when he was bitten by a fish,
he took its liver, heart and gall—as grim
incense to burn upon their wedding night.
Amid this smell of brine, she reached for him
the way a captured moth will flail for light.
But it was only when they knelt to pray
that her demon would finally fly away.

III.

That her demon would finally fly away,
Tobiah trusted. He would take the chance.
There's always something standing in the way,
waiting to kill the fantasy, romance.
There's always those who try to love you, try—
but who will leave, afraid to end up dead,
afraid to fight, to stay. And that is why
Tobiah could win Sarah, and behead
her demon. He knew death was in the deal,
but felt that she was worth it. That's the cost
of loving. Dying to yourself, you heal.
In giving up, you gain more than you lost.
A fish's gall is smeared upon your eyes,
and when the scales fall, you can see your prize.

How to Go Like Lazarus

I.

But what is in the way is always death.
The women dance, Lazarus, as you rise
among the bones, and then you take a breath
for the first time. Reborn, adjust your eyes
to filter light. Why fight it? All the skulls
around you smile. The rock is rolled away
from your tomb's entrance. Children shriek like gulls
and cry and laugh to see the stale bouquet
of you, dried flowers falling from your hands.
But all is beautiful to you. You see
each corpse around you rising, understand
the future, suddenly. And you foresee
skin wrapping around bones, the awkward dance
of resurrection, of a second chance.

II.

And when the scales fall, you can see your prize.
Your burial bands drop—your fish's scales.
For days you swam in nothingness, your eyes—
unseeing shells, and now the seaweed veils
have sunk down deep below. You've risen toward
the surface, to new life. You are untied
from shrouds of kelp. You breathe and are restored.
Your name is Lazarus, you rode the tide
of death to life. You'll die again someday.
But living is the art that you prefer.
Each time is better than the last, a way
to fight the masochist, the saboteur,
the voice inside that's taunting, casting stones—
because you want to dance among the bones.

How to Rise from the Dead

"Thus says the Lord God to these bones: 'See! I will bring spirit into you, that you may come to life. I will put sinews upon you, make flesh grow over you, cover you with skin, and put spirit in you so that you may come to life and know that I am the Lord.' I prophesied as I had been told, and even as I was prophesying I heard a noise; it was a rattling as the bones came together, bone joining bone." (E 37:5-7)

And like a funeral in New Orleans,
where jazz becomes synonymous with death
or like the painted skulls among the scenes
of Mexico's Day of the Dead—each breath
Ezekiel took as he prophesied
resounded over those dry bones and shook
them with God's heady music. Homicide
or natural cause, each skull could rise and look
at its old body with new eyes. What then?
Drum beat of bone, a mariachi dirge
of rattling. Spirit joining once again
to body sings first, then acts on the urge
to dance—scatter the marigolds of sleep,
then move its limbs, un-choreographed sweep.

Then move your limbs, un-choreographed sweep
of dance—scatter the marigolds of sleep.
The skull sings first, the bones then have the urge
to rattle. Spirit joining once again—

74

drum beat of bone, a mariachi dirge
for your old body, seen through new eyes. Then?
From natural cause, your song will rise and look
at life—God's heady music. Homicide
resounded over the dry bones and shook
Ezekiel's nerve, but he prophesied
like Mexico's Day of the Dead—each breath
bold like the painted skulls among the scenes
where jazz becomes synonymous with death—
and like a funeral in New Orleans.

III

Salome's Crown for John

"But at a birthday celebration for Herod, the daughter of Herodias performed a dance before the guests and delighted Herod so much that he swore to give her whatever she might ask for. Prompted by her mother, she said, 'Give me here on a platter the head of John the Baptist.'" (Mt 14:6-8)

I.

I've come to hate the way I danced. My arms
swaying to drum-beats were my call to war—
the way I challenged any woman's charms
and made a man see only me, want more
than what I showed through subtle turns of cloth—
until the more I moved, the more he swore
he'd have me—pin my body like a moth
against the floor. I've come to hate the chore
of teasing lust from strangers. There's a font
inside me where once there was just a door
I'd closed—though others thought it open. Want
can do that sort of thing—but I abhor
what I have done. I dammed the water's source.
I used the passion of my limbs as force.

II.

I used the passion of my limbs as force.
My mother nodded—but I heard the wails
when I asked for her wish. Then shame—remorse
became the fabric of my seven veils.
I close my eyes and see the prophet's head
upon the platter, mouth severed from breath.
If I had won my first request instead,
I'd have a bracelet, not a plate of death.
Why did I ask for it? Why use my lips
as trumpets sounding battle on one life?
I doubted that mere thrusting of my hips
could really raise or lower Herod's knife;
but wanted to find out if it were true
my motions could discomfit and subdue.

III.

My motions could discomfit and subdue
a man between the sheets, I knew. I'd won
a heart or ten, never a skull. Taboo—
to mention all the parts I've claimed. I'm done
dancing for hearts and heads, know what the brag
has cost. The night they served my severed wish,
I had just bathed. They took it from a bag—
held by the hair and placed it on a dish
beside my bed where just the night before
ripe pomegranates dropped their clotted seeds.
And I remembered their dark stains, the gore
of sweetness on my fingers. Those red beads
were what I saw when I first glimpsed the blood
staining the prophet's mouth—each speck, a bud.

IV.

Staining the prophet's mouth, each speck a bud—
I had imagined they would clean him first.
I told the guards to smooth away the blood
staining his beard. Trying to wash, submerse,
undo my wrong, I raised my still-wet sponge
to one of them, asked him to wipe the brow
of the Baptist. He laughed. I rose and plunged
my robe in water, rushed to disavow
my crime, reverse the stains. I tended him
with what I could. But his still-open eyes
were beautiful; their light had not yet dimmed.
I thought he had a lovely face—rough, wise,
and strong. His hair was gleaming, face was browned
and had a look of mercy I'd not found.

V.

He had a look of mercy I'd not found
in any man before. Not him, the brute—
the warmonger. This head—beautiful, round—
the coin I'd won—was not a cut bud. Shoot
of new life, though severed, I wish I'd known
him when he lived; then I might have lived, too.
I would have followed John. He would have shown
me uses for my dance. The old tattoo
of sorrow on my skin he would have drowned
within the Jordan. Naked, then reborn,
I would have given him myself, and crowned
him as my king. Why then was I the thorn?
I called to God to come remove the tray—
to make him whole again, take him away.

VI.

To make him whole again, take him away
from me. This was my prayer the night I'd danced
for death. I asked that this prophet of day—
of light, sent to his end by one entranced—
could somehow be put back together. But
my plea not yet completed, there he stood
before me. Herod. Licked his lips, then shut
the door. *Dance for me, Salome, you're good—*
Why do you shake your head, refuse a king?
I gave you what you wanted, it's your turn.
Why did you not request a dress, a ring?
You are a strange one. Even so, I burn
for you. And what you will not give, I'll take.
Where is your power now? Look how you shake.

VII.

Where is *your* power now? Look how *you* shake,
I said to Herod as he told me, *Dance.* You
were not the first man here who came to take
me for himself. I'm owned first by a Jew,
a desert wanderer, a homeless priest.
But Herod laughed. *He's dead, and now you fall*
in love with what you danced to kill? At least
explain this—how his head holds you in thrall.
I answered: Some of his blood smeared on me
as I was tending him. Now there's a font
inside me where was once an aimless sea.
I was baptized tonight, and now I want
to love what I have killed, sent to the knife.
I dance for what I lost. I dance for life.

The Marionette's Ascent

Acknowledgments:

Dappled Things: "In the Church: A Mirror Crown"
"Pinocchio"
"The Black Tear"
(published as "The Marionette Considers
the Jester Doll")

The Lyric: "Labor as Play"

The National Review: "The Teddy Bear"

The Seventh Quarry: "The Conjoined Feet"
(Published as "The Doll Comments on
the Army Men")
"The Marionette's Manifesto"

Umbrella: "Jack-in-the-Box"

I. Prologue

The Marionette's Manifesto

I.

I'd like to shake your hand. Come, pull my string.
It's nice to meet you. Call me Marion.
I've dropped the "ette." I'm never one to cling
to lame conventions. Libertarian—
that's me. I always choose the things I can.
My smile never fades; my eyes don't blink.
I'm like a painted Bodhisattva—scan
each audience for worship, laughter—think:
what brought them here to gaze? Watch how I twirl.
The wooden dance is beautiful, absurd.
I move for the Manipulator, whirl—
within a cage of strings. I am the bird
whose flight depends upon a coop of strands—
dangling from the Manipulator's hands.

II.

Dangling from the Manipulator's hands,
I'm born. The other puppets think he's God.
He made me. But this caught doll understands
that even though he makes me bow and nod,
chose auburn for my hair, blue for my eyes—
he didn't make himself. Someone made him.
He wasn't always there. I've been called wise
by some; faithless by others—but this hymn
of skepticism is my silent song.
God might be in the trees; trees gave the wood
that gave me life. I don't think it is wrong,
without a sacred image to find good
and holiness in roots and leaves and trunks.
But maybe they're not gods—just swaying monks.

III.

But maybe they're not gods—just swaying monks.
Does wind manipulate them, make them thrash?
Whoever made the air that makes trees dunk
their leaves into the lake; each shifting crash
of pressure—high to low, I think that one
designed freedom in order—just the way
the sunset colors vary but the sun
sets every night. Just so, my strings, each day,
allowing me to move. Oh, ordered flight.
Passion can soar within constraints. And who
on earth can be completely free? Each night
she'll tire, need to rest. My point of view:
Free will is choosing what you can. The rest?
It's dancing through restraint—that is the test.

IV.

It's dancing through restraint that is the test.
It's how you handle what you can't control.
For you, perhaps an unexpected guest,
the pain of loss, failure to meet a goal—
for me, it is the bridle tug of limbs.
Go with the tug and not against and then
the dance is beautiful. The process dims
compared to the result. And that's why men
don't readily quit jobs that let them dance.
Some say: don't bite the beak to spite the hen;
so I won't bite my strings off—wound romance,
allure. For all these reasons, I won't bite.
(I don't have teeth.) That's why I seem polite.

V.

I don't have teeth. That's why I seem polite
and so the spectators might think me mild.
But this evaluation isn't right.
I am opinionated, even wild;
and there is no string made to pull my mind.
Past my archaic smile, ribboned hair,
the structured, ordered way I was designed,
my face holds under pressure as crowds stare.
But when my rigid feet strike on the stage,
listen for rage and passion in the sound.
I have no legs; the shoes, part of my cage,
are worn by strings. Wooden, they hit the ground
in bold morse code, an auditory braille—
each sound, my manifesto as I flail.

VI.

Each sound, my manifesto as I flail—
I am Lady Houdini. Watch me fly
through the constraints that seem a kind of jail,
fashioning art in limits. I untie
a dance from the Manipulator's hands.
The challenge always makes me feel at home.
Although my motions follow set commands,
the dance is still my own. Sometimes a poem
surprises its own poet. Painters know
the happy accidents their brushes make.
Much in this way, each well-applauded show
is partly the Manipulator's shake
but partly how I move, how I respond.
I am the rabbit summoned by the wand.

VII.

I am the rabbit summoned by the wand,
the smoke-and-mirror act behind the screen.
(That is our puppeteer-and-puppet bond.)
I need his finger motions to be seen;
his strong hands help me move. He needs my form
to show his skill. I am the instrument,
and he, the music-maker. We perform—
together. Sometimes there's an argument
within me: which of us is needed more?
The cellist or the cello? They are one—
one body joined in music. To ignore
the daylight is to disregard the sun.
I'm tugged; but every strand is like a wing.
I'd like to shake your hand. Come, pull my string.

II. Purgatorio

In the Nursery

Somehow I wound up on this wooden chair—
my strings are wrapped around its arms. I think
this place is purgatory for the bear
whose stuffing hangs out loosely from his pink
stomach and sides. The doll whose head fell off
is clearly in a ring of hell. But some
toys seem delighted even as I scoff
and tell them of my life on stage. This slum
of drool, with striped walls colored like a clown
smells like animal crackers, sour milk.
I will describe the others. All around
this room are scattered toys, not of my ilk.
My eyes travel like pilgrims through this place
teeming with stringless puppets lacking grace.

The Teddy Bear

That is a human curiosity—
endear what might destroy you in the wild.
Give children emblems of ferocity
to cuddle when they're frightened, sad or riled.
Take what is fierce and form it from tame cloth.
Forget that in the wild it would bite.
Forget its claws; forget its teeth, like froth
glinting against the ocean of the night.
Then stuff it up with cotton, as you stuff
all that is raw and frightening in life;
in nursery rhymes, reducing fears to fluff—
reach for a bear to calm a child's strife.
A bear and not a mouse to cling to, hold—
illusion that the fierce can be controlled.

Jack-in-the-Box

Redundant. The first time he popped, I jumped.
He laughed. Jack is an ass. A giddy fool.
He shook a little, side to side, then slumped
back into that preposterous footstool
he calls his box. I wish it were his tomb.
And then the music, if it can be called
by such a name, begins again. The room
is filled with tinny noise. I am appalled
each time I hear it. Like a music box
about to break chimed with the ice cream truck.
I'd like to enlist chains and sturdy locks
to keep Jack down. I'd like him to get stuck.
He rises up like heartburn. Fear? Or fun?
What is his point? And when will he be done?

The Trolls

There's ten of them, at least. They wear no clothes.
Bright hair stands on each scalp as though a flame.
Like me, they have no eyelids; but repose
is just what they require. There's a game
they play. It is a staring contest. Yawn.
I liked to play that when I was young, when
the puppets with eyelids would play till dawn
trying to win. I always did. Therein
I drew some pride, until I realized eyes
should have the humane option to be closed.
I see too much. I wait for the disguise
of night to shroud my constant gaze. Composed,
console myself that I am not a troll—
naked with neon hair out of control.

The Blonde Doll

There's just something about her. She is small
and thin, more like a woman than a child.
She has so many clothes and shoes that sprawl
around the nursery. I am beguiled
and jealous when I look at her. My dress
is never changed, and worst of all my form
is flat and plain—she has those puzzling breasts
and though her personality's lukewarm,
her intellect pastel, I watch her man—
the man-doll she is matched with; he's polite,
gorgeous—but plastic. No male in my clan
of puppets was a looker. They're too bright
with red cheeks, lips and chins. But they have wood
for crotches—the way every boy-doll should.

Labor as Play

The favorite toys are labor in disguise:
a wooden tool kit, baby doll and pram—
a plastic lawnmower. And this defies
my reason. This is ludicrous, a sham.
A kitchen set complete with plastic food,
with pots and pans, an apron, white chef's hat?
Adults came up with this; their motives shrewd.
Give children work disguised as play and that
will guarantee adult proclivity.
It fascinates me, as the children mime
their work, adults seek creativity—
a yoga class, ceramics, extra time
for taking trips to beaches by the sea—
while children practice pouring cups of tea.

Still Life: Potato with Hat and Glasses

This plastic starchy tuber of a head,
resembling a male because it's bald
and has a mustache—he's a thoroughbred.
Ancestors? All potato-dolls. He's sprawled
across the nursery. Glasses, hat and arms
in different places. He can be a flirt.
It's odd: somehow he thinks that he has charms.
I dealt him a rejoinder. He was hurt
and said that he'd no longer wear his eyes—
I was too beautiful, he said, and he
could not bear my refusal. All his tries
got him nowhere with me. But don't you see,
I said, you're just a head. A plastic head.
A puppet likes a body in her bed.

Slinking Around

All right; I will admit I had a crush
on something otherworldly. I'm ashamed
to think about it. What the hell. A rush
of passion still sears through me when he's named.
The silver macaroni, he was called.
He freely moved—without the use of strings.
I saw him springing, and I was enthralled.
He moved across my lap and told me things—
I liked his lack of face, his smooth, slick glaze.
He was a curl of gleaming water, strong
but bendable in all the best of ways.
We hid our time together; it was wrong.
One day he said he didn't like my strings.
I told him he could shove off on his springs.

The Conjoined Feet

There have to be a hundred of these men.
Tiny and green—to them I'm like a hulk.
At first I saw them from a distance, when
they lay in one large pile, strength in bulk.
They looked so much like surfers, feet attached
to each straight board. They're military men
in miniature. Battlefields dispatched
to nurseries. It's wartime for the playpen.
How interesting—soldiers posed as toys.
Conjoined feet pointed toward the fight and hands
holding long guns. Teach little girls and boys
of strategy, of following commands.
Hint of what lurks beyond the playroom walls—
war's immobilities—bullies and brawls.

The Black Tear

The ones in porcelain with eyes that close—
the ones who wear long gowns of silk, and stare
perched on the playroom shelf, standing in rows—
the perfect dolls who show no wear and tear—
the ones with small and dainty fingered hands—
expressionless, they laugh at me, the way
my strings are knotted. One, though, understands;
her face was made to always show dismay—
the bright doll in the pale blue jester's cap,
a painted black tear ever on her cheek,
she's just like me. We're both in the same trap—
the audience assumes that we are weak.
She with the tear that's always there, and me,
hanging like branches from a swaying tree.

Body's Editor

I.

Telepathy is how. That is the way
I speak to other dolls without a tongue—
with only lips, red as a raw filet.
But not so with the humans. As the young,
small children ask for stories before sleep,
their mother enters. She reads—eyes and lips
dancing together—rhymes. *Baa, baa, black sheep,*
cows jumping over moons. Then the eclipse—
she turns the light off. I want to tell her:
return me to your brother, he's the one
who made me. I don't know why he'd transfer
my ownership to toddlers, leave me, run
away. I'd tired of him, too, but he
was mine, or I was his, carved from his tree—

II.

A tree that fell during a hurricane—
I'm made of lightning pine, he always said.
I'd take the stage, he'd move my limbs like rain
shaking beneath the cloud of him. His head
was like the sun I couldn't see, beyond
the darkness up above. Ahead, stage light
would blind my lidless eyes. I had a bond
with the Manipulator, but my fright
was of the staring audience—appease
the restless popcorn-munchers. Then one day,
I learned to block them out, like a strip tease
performed by one alone. I was his prey,
Manipulator was my predator,
or if not that, my body's editor.

Puppeteer

And so, I came to love him, or at least
to play the part. Yet stranger things have been.
I've heard the mother telling of the beast
a beauty fell in love with. My chagrin
in loving a manipulator pales
compared to fairy stories filled with pain.
I'll have to bring perspective to these tales.
This will be my new project, my campaign:
to tell my own yarns, all my storied rhymes—
my way. I'll call them Marion-vignettes.
I've played these stories out a hundred times.
I will not try to tinge them with regret.
My body's editor has left me here.
He is an evil, heartless puppeteer.

Pinocchio

I.

It's true I came to love him, or at least
to fantasize about him. After all,
he was one of my kind. My awe increased
to hear he was made real—went from a thrall
of cherry wood to the free will of flesh.
And like a girl in poverty who reads
of Cinderella's fortune, this refreshed
my lust for freedom, movement. All my needs,
desires were projected onto him—
Pinocchio's great triumph. Then love turned.
My admiration morphed to envy. Slim,
slim chance I had of being real. I'd learned.
I'd never been rescued, despite my tries.
No cricket-conscience could undo my lies.

II.

I tell myself too many to keep track.
Each day I say I could get up and walk
if I just wanted to. My limbs are slack
and always are—without someone to stalk
my every movement with a push or tug.
Where's my blue fairy, bringing me to life?
Where's Jiminy to guide me from my smug
naiveté, my solitude and strife?
Gladly would I be swallowed by the whale
if it just meant that I could find someone
as faithful as Gepetto. In the tale,
he treats that long-nosed liar like a son.
And if a maker loves what he has made,
it grows, however long it is delayed.

Gethsemane

My body's editor has left me here
among the playroom toys; I'm still alone.
Though I should be asleep, I overhear
the bedtime stories, every whispered tone
the mother murmurs gently. And last night
she talked about a man who was afraid,
forsaken. He was also God. Not right
that in the garden where this Jesus prayed
his friends all fell asleep. He'd understand—
I'd like to sit with him beneath the moon
of his drear garden, tell him what's been planned.
My body's editor will claim me soon.
Tomorrow, I'll be going on the road.
The puppeteer's remembered what I'm owed.

The String Holder

He is an evil, heartless puppeteer—
my object of affection and disdain.
I am the Sutradhara. Though I fear
and crave the way he makes me move, the pain
of his manipulation and his hold,
the pride in how I soar beneath his hands—
it's my turn now. Bring vibrant marigolds,
drape me in silks of red and let the strands
I dangle from be strung with jewels and beads.
My body's all in strings; it's full of lines—
poetic lines—as strong as river reeds.
I've taken power back through my designs—
the henna-bold narration of my verse.
I hold the strings and spin bright tales—diverse.

*A Sutradhara is the narrator within Hindu dance-drama, and is considered
important due to his role of holding the story together. Sutradhara literally means
"the string holder."*

III. Inferno

The Sutradhara

I.

The Sutradhara enters. He's the one
who pulls my strings. I'm lying on this bed
in some unknown motel. It has been fun
performing with him, as he moves each thread—
it's like I know already what he'll do.
We're on the road, performing thirty shows
in thirty cities. There have been a slew
of stages, star-hot lights and raucous rows
of gapers. And tonight, my body slack,
he's draped me on the bed, not on the chair.
He takes his shirt off; I study his back.
He sits down on the bed, begins to stare.
Even without his touch, I feel his hold.
I realize that I'm still being controlled.

II.

I realize that I'm still being controlled,
but suddenly wish I was made of flesh.
I want to sit up, reach out and unfold
his limbs. I'd make him move—and then enmesh
his body in the net of my embrace.
He's the Manipulator, but lately
he calls himself my Sutradhara. Grace
and passion tinge those vowels and greatly
increase the dreams I have of his sure touch.
The poses: like a Kama Sutra dance—
that he arranges, all to bring me much
delight. He's like a lover, each advance
is to ensure this girl of wood and strings
knows what a life of such warm contact brings.

III.

Know what a life of such warm contact brings?
I'm always, always waiting for the tease
he'll make me dance, the way my wood and strings
will bend the ways he wants. I'm his trapeze.
He is the acrobat. I will not lie—
I sometimes like the way he makes me sway,
other times I resent each binding tie,
the way he always puts me on display.
So anyway, I'm here now on this bed,
oddly surprised when his hand moves toward me.
He reaches for my arm, I feel each thread
of string and grain of wood within me plea
to be touched more. But he just smoothes my dress.
My fantasy continues nonetheless.

IV.

My fantasy continues nonetheless.
I wish I were a girl of flesh instead.
Then I could tell him how I feel, confess.
Instead of distant tugs from overhead,
I'd feel his his pull on skin instead of wood.
A doll is made for touch, and I'm part doll.
I'd like to be held. It would do me good
to be cradled and given time to loll
in someone's arms. Each pointer on my hand
extends. That's just the way that I was carved.
I wish my puppeteer would understand
I always point to hands. It's like I'm starved
for touch. And I'm no baby doll. I want
affection beating, drum-like, while I flaunt.

V.

Affection beating, drum-like, while I flaunt
the twirls of my design, how I beguile.
The Sutradhara made my face to haunt.
My mask: permanent makeup, cryptic smile.
There's always a gold ribbon in my hair.
I can be posed and draped in countless ways.
I listen well—enticing! And I dare
a man to look at me without some praise.
I dare him not to want to move my strings.
How can he keep from savoring the might
I make him feel, inspiring him to things—
bending the ways he wants to in the night.
I know I tend to dream, romanticize.
I think it's normal that I fantasize.

VI.

I think it's normal that I fantasize
about the man who holds me in such sway.
I justify his moves, romanticize
his motivations, as he gets his way
night after night. He dangles me and hides
in darkness, while I bend, perform, display
the comedy or drama he decides.
I sometimes dream of inverting our play,
holding him captive underneath my touch.
I'd make the Sutradhara writhe and bow,
and then I'd teach him love. I know that much.
This is my fantasy—I'll tell it now.
(For a marionette, it's pretty bold),
I realize that I'm still being controlled.

VII.

I realize that I'm still being controlled;
even without his touch, I feel his hold.
He sits down on the bed, begins to stare,
then takes his shirt off. I study his back.
He's draped me on the bed, not on the chair.
He's gaping at me now, my body slack
from stages, star-hot lights and raucous rows
in thirty cities; there have been a slew.
We're on the road, performing thirty shows.
It's like I know already what he'll do,
performing with him, as he moves each thread—
in some unknown motel. It has been fun.
Who pulls my strings? I'm lying on his bed.
The Sutradhara enters. He's the one.

IV. Paradiso

"Take this cup away from me, but not what I will but what You will." (Mk 14:36)

In the Church: A Mirror Crown

I.

I've come here to confess. That must be why
after the puppet show was over, done,
my unstrung hero left me here to die
a puppet death of solitude—a gun
to splinter all my grains of wood to prayer.
He always knew I needed crowds and light.
I'm propped up in a pew. This is his dare.
But leaving me alone here wasn't right.
It's strange to feel the absence of each tug
upon my strings. Manipulator's gone.
I sense a creeping feeling, like a bug—
intimidating beauty, like a swan.
There's something vital in the silence here.
It's doubt, or faith. It's trust. Or is it fear?

II.

It's doubt, or faith. It's trust. Or is it fear?
What is it that I feel when I'm alone?
Dependency has marked my whole career.
In all this stillness, there's an undertone,
susurrous music of identity.
What am I when I do not move or dance?
I'm tangled up, a dumb non-entity.
Not even Sutradhara could enhance
my negativity, my lack of hope.
Only the One who made all life could know
the trees I came from, and the broader scope,
the seeds of what imagined I would grow.
Tonight I want to go back to my roots,
escape this strung-up tree, my buried shoots.

III.

Escape this strung-up tree with buried shoots—
flee from the cold eyes watching me perform.
Perhaps he felt like this among the roots,
between night's petals, huddled to keep warm.
Among his sleeping friends, the garden bed
so dark with dread. I look up at him now.
He hangs here in this church above my head.
He moves me without strings to make a vow.
I promise: here I'll sit, all night with him;
I've finally found a use for lidless eyes.
I see that he is nailed there, limb by limb
attached to wood, but by such different ties.
All this, and he went willingly. He chose.
Death's own marionette, until he rose.

IV.

Death's own marionette, until he rose,
each person was a puppet strung to death:
what this crucifix teaches, what it shows.
True freedom comes in honoring each breath.
I feel the air against my wood, my dust.
I'm glad the Sutradhara left me here.
He always pulled at me, challenged my trust.
He sometimes made me think I needed fear.
Remember where I come from? Mystery plays.
Marionette means little Mary, right?
Always, above me, there's a cross that stays:
cruciform wood, to hold my limbs for flight.
A cross was always over Mary's head.
In nightmares, she would wake and find him dead.

V.

In nightmares, she would wake and find him dead.
She worried even when he was a child,
nestled the sleeping boy below her head.
Fearing the pain He'd face, worries compiled.
Umbilical cord was the Virgin's string
connecting her to her One. I suppose
she's like me: cross above her, bonds that cling—
The only difference is that Mary chose.
I see the stories there, in that stained glass.
I've stayed awake all night, pale morning light
annunciating this, my private Mass.
Marion's found a home here; this feels right.
Only a God nailed to a cross could know
my smaller burden—suffering the show.

VI.

My smaller burden—suffering each show.
There—propped against the font, an instrument.
It's that large-bodied, stringed puppet I know
to be a cello, music immanent—
I hear it in my thoughts. Here's what I want:
to recognize the good in how I'm carved.
I see the good in sound holes, tunes that haunt.
I see beauty in bridges, varnish. Starved
for goodness in myself, I just see red.
Synthetic red hair, painted blush, dark as
a realization: the scroll is my head.
The fingerboard's my neck. My body's jazz.
I sense it now. I'd thought my hopes were frayed.
I am the instrument. I must be played.

VII.

I am the instrument. I must be played.
It's true that motion is my music, dance.
I'm willing to sit here forever, trade
this life of needing hands to make me prance.
Death to dependency—yet if I'm grabbed
by the Manipulator, I will go,
freer than I was heretofore. If nabbed,
then that will be my sacrifice. I'll grow.
Willingly, I will face the stage again.
If that's the cup that will not pass from me,
I think I can accept that. That's not pain
compared to sacrifice nailed to a tree.
At first, I thought I'd been left here to die.
I've come here to confess; that must be why.

VIII.

I've come here to confess; that must be why.
At first, I thought I'd been left here to die.
Compared to sacrifice nailed to a tree,
I think that I can handle that—the pain.
If that's the cup that will not pass from me,
willingly, I will face the stage again.
That will be my choice: sacrifice. I'll grow
freer than I was heretofore. If nabbed
by the Manipulator, I will go.
Death to dependency—yet if I'm grabbed
I'll go back to the hands that make me prance.
I'm willing to sit here forever, trade
my motion for hushed music. But I'll dance
again. An instrument, I must be played.

IX.

I am the instrument. I must be played.
I sense it now. I'd thought my hopes were frayed.
The fingerboard's my neck. My body's jazz.
A realization: the scroll is my head;
synthetic red hair, painted blush-dark. As
for goodness in myself, I just see red.
I find beauty in bridges, varnish-starved;
perceive the good in sound holes, tunes that haunt.
To recognize the good in how I'm carved,
I must direct my thoughts. Here's what I want:
to be a cello—music immanent,
large-bodied, wooden, stringed puppet I know
is propped at the church font—an instrument.
My smaller burden—suffering the show.

X.

My smaller burden—suffering the show—
only a God nailed to a cross could know.
Marion's found a home here; it feels right
annunciating this, my private Mass.
I've stayed awake all night, till morning light.
I see the stories there, in that stained glass.
The only difference is that Mary chose.
She's like me, cross above her, bonds that cling—
connecting her to her One. I suppose
umbilical cord was the Virgin's string.
Fearing the pain he'd face, worries compiled.
Nestled, a sleeping boy below her head—
she worried even when he was a child.
In nightmares, she would wake and find him dead.

XI.

In nightmares, she would wake and find him dead.
A cross was always over Mary's head:
cruciform wood, to hold the limbs for flight.
Always, above me, there's a cross that stays.
Marionette means little Mary. Right?
Remember where I come from? Mystery plays.
He sometimes made me think I needed fear.
He always pulled at me, challenged my trust:
I'm glad the Sutradhara left me here.
I feel the air against my wood, my dust.
True freedom comes in honoring each breath.
What this crucifix teaches, what it shows:
each person was a puppet strung to death,
death's own marionette, until he rose.

XII.

Death's own marionette, until he rose.
All this, and he went willingly. He chose.
Attached to wood, but by such different ties,
I see that he is nailed there, limb by limb.
I've finally found a use for lidless eyes.
I promise I'll sit here all night with him.
He moves me without strings to make a vow.
He hangs there in this church above my head.
So dark with dread, I look up at him now.
Among his sleeping friends, the garden bed
between night's petals, huddled to keep warm,
He felt this way that night among the roots:
Flee from the cold eyes watching me perform;
escape this strung-up tree with buried shoots.

XIII.

Escape this strung-up tree with buried shoots—
tonight I want to go back to my roots,
the seeds of what imagined me, and grow
the trees I came from, and the broader scope.
Only the One who made all life could know
my negativity, my lack of hope
not even Sutradhara could enhance—
I'm tangled up, a dumb non-entity.
What am I when I do not move or dance?
Susurrous music of identity.
In all this stillness, there's an undertone—
dependency has marked my whole career.
What is it that I feel when I'm alone?
It's doubt, or faith. It's trust. Or is it fear?

XIV.

It's doubt, or faith. It's trust. Or is it fear?
There's something vital in the silence here—
intimidating beauty, like a swan.
I sense a creeping feeling, like a bug
upon my strings. Manipulator's gone.
It's nice to feel the absence of each tug,
but leaving me alone here wasn't right.
I'm propped up in a pew. This is his dare.
He always knew I needed crowds and light.
To splinter all my grains of wood to prayer,
a puppet death of solitude—a gun,
my unstrung hero left me here to die
after the puppet show was over, done.
I've come here to confess. That must be why.

Afterword:

This double volume may be seen as two poetic testaments. *A Ship to Hold the World* would, of course, be the Old Testament and *The Marionette's Ascent* would be the New. The two poetic testaments are joined by the heartbeat of iambic pentameter in most cases, but form in all. This rhythm is the Ruah—the breath and spirit joining the collection as a whole.

A Ship to Hold the World takes its name from the title poem of the collection in honor of Noah. Just as a womb holds the ocean of life for a fetus, Noah's ship held the only remaining life, all the world, while the tempest raged and that world was tossed. One can scarcely blame Noah for his drunkenness, as he grappled with the enormity of all who had lost their lives, and the survivor's guilt of being among the very few left. I imagine Noah's family, their various personalities tested by long days tossed in an ark while the seas raged and the animals growled and whimpered. I imagine the arguments and irritations—even the jealousies, that must have arisen amidst the close quarters; all while they grappled with fear and sorrow and guilt.

A Ship to Hold the World is an ark in its own way: holding the various emotions and stories of some the most compelling voices from Scripture. A world of human experience awaits within: from Cain's bitterness, Delilah's shame and Job's anguish to Bathsheba's passion and Salome's remorse. In "Moses," the very basket that held the endangered infant also becomes an ark, a symbol of God's mercy, a compelling reason that the exhausted Moses forges ahead in the desert. To develop the sense of the timelessness of each of these characters, I wrote some of the poems as though they could be recited in Biblical times whilst others I cast in a contemporary tone. These famous characters are archetypes of emotions we all experience in one form or another. It may be said that each of us is an ark, a ship holding a world of potential. In the end, it remains to be seen which contents each of us will bring safely ashore.

I tried to inhabit each character I wrote, whether it meant poetically dwelling with unhinged envy, shame, forgiveness or love. The emotional spectrum within the poems is wide and all-encompassing. Often, a character experiences conflicting emotions, such as Delilah's defense and regret of her betrayal, or Job's feeling of abandonment by and love for God. I was reminded, through writing these poems, of the myriad seeming contradictions encompassed in the human heart. In the words of Walt Whitman: "Do I contradict myself? Very well, then, I contradict myself. I am large, I contain multitudes."

A Ship to Hold the World begins with Eden's Serpent, and comes full-circle in an ouroboros (from the Greek, an ancient symbol of the serpent eating its own tail, or in this case, "tale,") to again encounter Eden's Serpent and then find renewal in the closing poems that each, in different ways, summon a dance. Lazarus's second chance at life is celebrated with the desire to "dance among the bones," while Salome's atonement and newfound love of John the Baptist leads her to seek to "dance for what [she] lost...for life."

Why end with images of dance? It is its own covenant: a physical sign awaiting the redemption it foresees. When a ship that holds the world finally reaches shore, and all the various souls get out and put their tired feet into the sand, a dance is a deeply symbolic, whole-bodied act of joy and trust.

What do poems written as dramatic narratives in ancient voices from Scripture have in common with the poems written in the voice of a brash marionette? The ship holds a world of timeless human experience, but is missing one thing: the fulfillment of the scriptures in redemption. That is where *The Marionette's Ascent* enters. We meet Marion, a highly-opinionated puppet "everyman." I use that word to include both men and women in its embrace and because the character's experience is universal, and the concept of an "everyman" in literature is a key component in Dante and many other of the great classic works I admire. Like Dante, Marion travels through Purgatory, Hell and Heaven in the forms of a nursery, a hotel room and a church.

Just as A Ship to Hold the World ends with dance, *The Marionette's Ascent* begins with a dance. "The wooden dance is beautiful, absurd." It continues, "Free will is choosing what you can. The rest?/ It's dancing through restraint—that is the test." We do not have the ability to choose everything that happens to us in life. What we can choose, however, is how we respond.

As the characters in *A Ship to Hold the World* did before her, and, indeed, as those who contain multitudes may do, Marion seems to contradict herself at times. Sometimes, the strings that bind her limbs signify a blessing, one that gives her a chance to show grace under pressure: "Oh, ordered flight. Passion can soar within constraints/...Free will is choosing what you can. The rest?/ It's dancing through restraint—that is the test." Later, the restraints are a curse. "Each day I say I could get up and walk/ if I just wanted to. My limbs are slack/ and always are—without someone to stalk/ my every movement with a push or tug." This is why poetry can be a spiritual experience: its ability to, through metaphor, represent the state of BOTH AND. For example, Marion is BOTH shackled AND free.

She contradicts herself where the puppeteer is concerned, seeing him as "an evil, heartless puppeteer — / My object of affection and disdain." Sometimes she loves the way he makes her move: "the pride in how I soar beneath his hands," but at other times, "I was his prey,/ Manipulator was my predator." In times of hatred she calls him "Manipulator," with a capital M. The figure of the Manipulator is that of evil incarnate within her journey. However, when she desires him, Marion claims he has dubbed himself "Sutradhara" and is all too willing to refer to him that way.

The first appearance of the word "Sutradhara" actually occurs earlier in the collection, and refers to Marion herself, in the poem entitled, "The String Holder." This is the last poem of Marion's Purgatorio, just after she distracts herself from thoughts of

Gethsemane with: "the puppeteer's remembered what I'm owed." In an emboldened voice, Marion asserts, "I am the Sutradhara," evoking the Hindu narrator of a dance drama who literally "holds the strings" of the story together. She calls for marigolds and silks to be draped around her form as she celebrates: "My body's all in strings; it's full of lines—/ poetic lines as strong as river reeds./ I've taken power back through my designs..." When the puppet-master, the Manipulator, begins to refer to *himself* as Sutradhara, it is a show of how the enemy twists and bends something that might have set us free to, instead, hold us in thrall.

Sutradhara is evocative of "Kama Sutra." In Sanskrit, Kama means "love" and Sutra means "string." "The poses: like a Kama Sutra dance—/ that he arranges, all to bring me much/ delight." Her Hell is unrequited lust for the abusive puppeteer, the state of a soul choosing the very worst for itself. If there is grace present it is here: "I realize that I'm still being controlled." Perspective has not been entirely lost.

While the Purgatorio is the toy room, rife with characters that annoy, disgust, interest, amuse and even empathize with Marion (whose bawdy and brash side is in full bloom here), and the Inferno is the hotel room with the half-naked Sutradhara, Paradiso is found when Marion, after performing in a show given at a church, is left behind, "propped up in a pew." At first, being there alone feels like death: "a puppet death of solitude—a gun/ to splinter all my grains of wood to prayer. He always knew I needed crowds and light" she says, contradicting herself again, as she earlier declares her fear of the very "restless popcorn munchers." Her discomfort in the "vital silence" and darkness of the church recalls the experience of Elijah in "The Whisper." "Do not sit still for long, or what you fear—/ it will come. When you're still, it will appear." Marion's experience of this is "intimidating beauty." This is Marion's authentic encounter with the numinous, the *mysterium tremendum*: that sense of closeness to the divine mystery that leaves one overwhelmed, even frightened.

The theme of free will continues as Marion beholds a figure of the crucified Christ hanging high above from the church ceiling. She realizes the poignant similarity: a body hanging from a wooden cross. She sees the story of his sacrificial death in the stained glass. "All this, and he went willingly. He chose." We arrive once more at the essential component: choice.

Marion later realizes a connection to Christ's mother, Mary. "Marionette means little Mary, right?/ Always, above me, there's a cross that stays:/ cruciform wood, to hold my limbs for flight./ A cross was always over Mary's head./ In nightmares, she would wake and find Him dead." Again, the essential component of Mary is her choice. "I suppose/ she's like me, cross above her, bonds that cling— / The only difference is that Mary chose."

Marion's journey culminates in two ways. First, she finds a blessing in the lidless eyes she complains of in "Trolls," part of Purgatorio: "Eyes/ should have the humane option to be closed." Now, in Paradiso, she has "finally found a use for lidless eyes," which is to keep awake with Christ in Gethsemane: "I promise:

here I'll sit, all night with Him." Though her body is not within her control, her will is. Marion could be physically rooted to her seat, but if she did not will the love and companionship she offers, her proximity would be of no value.

Secondly, Marion decides she prefers the lack of motion, a frozen-limbed life, to the life of performing under the Manipulator's control. Yet, she accepts, "if I'm grabbed/ by the Manipulator, I will go,/ freer than I was heretofore. If nabbed,/ then that will be my sacrifice." Indeed, her will is at work once again. She dreads a return to the life of having her limbs tugged and pulled by a puppeteer, but if she must, then she decides to see it as her sacrifice, given in love. This is how Marion is transformed by grace and seeks to imitate Christ in both his suffering and the hope of resurrection. After all, Marion has finally felt truly understood: "Only a God nailed to a cross could know/ my smaller burden—suffering the show." The only one who ever gave Marion any sense of compassion before this moment was the jester doll in the toy room, who is reminiscent of Mary, Queen of Sorrows: "the bright doll in the pale blue...She with the tear that's always there..." Like Mary, Marion's assent is her ascent.

Some readers have asked me if the symbol of the puppeteer represents God. I must emphatically state that he does not. God could never be represented as a puppeteer, since He has given the gift of free will, and always lets us choose. Symbolically speaking, to be a marionette— to have a puppeteer— is to be under the sway of the enemy, one who would enjoy making a soul bend and twist the way he wants us to. Is each of us at times entrapped like a marionette, dancing to another's tune? Inevitably, yes. But as Marion reminds, "It's dancing through restraint that is the test."

This may be obvious, but I don't think there's any harm in stating it: I find no inherent fault or evil in an actual (non-symbolic) puppeteer. That is to say, someone who makes and operates toy puppets has a potentially fine vocation in delighting children and adults alike. It's the puppeteer as archetype, as symbol, that is the negation of free will.

I never did like marionettes. Perhaps this is because they are symbols of restraint and subjugation and the symbolism was at work at me even when I didn't notice. In any case, when I was a very young child, I was given one. It was a clown with a painted face, red cotton-ball buttons and a striped suit. I pitied it tremendously, not only for its strings, but for how frequently I (with some guilt) got them knotted. I am glad I had this toy as a child, as it gave me a clearer knowledge of the marionette form. I now have a special fondness for marionettes. Walking around in someone else's (wooden) shoes tends to have the effect of bringing understanding and ideally, empathy. Marion's ever-present strings remind me of the sufferings and sacrifices of each of our lives and, ultimately, of the cost of redemption.

—Annabelle Moseley
November, 2014

Acknowledgments

With gratitude to Joshua Hren, editor and publisher of Wiseblood Books, for his faith in my work, his support of my manuscripts: *A Ship to Hold the World* and *The Marionette's Ascent*, and his visionary publication of them as a double volume. I would like to thank copy editor Genevieve Cunningham for her assistance as the manuscript was prepared for publication. I am grateful to Dominic Heisdorf for his beautiful cover art and design. It was a delight to witness his talent at work: from my rather challenging request for a visual joining of my poetic depictions of God's salvation and love (a ship holding a world, a marionette strung from the masts,) to the realization of such a powerfully rendered image. Finally, I acknowledge gratitude to photographer Belenna Lauto, who showed me a series of photos she had taken of a red-haired, brightly made-up marionette. I had never much liked marionettes, and so I challenged myself to write one poem on the subject of a stringed puppet, thinking I would be lucky to write five lines. Before I knew it, the "Marionette's Manifesto" had poured forth, which led very quickly to the whole book, and in the end, a new affinity for marionettes.

45122191R00088

Made in the USA
Middletown, DE
24 June 2017